Options Trading

How To Get From Zero To Six Figures With Options Trading

JONATHAN S. WALKER

Copyright © 2017 Jonathan S. Walker

All rights reserved.

DEDICATION

I dedicate this book to my two beautiful children and my loving wife who have been nothing short of being my light and joy throughout the years.

Copyright 2017 by Jonathan S. Walker - All rights reserved.

The following eBook is reproduced below with the goal of providing information that is as accurate and reliable as possible. Regardless, purchasing this eBook can be seen as consent to the fact that both the publisher and the author of this book are in no way experts on the topics discussed within and that any recommendations or suggestions that are made herein are for entertainment purposes only. Professionals should be consulted as needed prior to undertaking any of the action endorsed herein.

This declaration is deemed fair and valid by both the American Bar Association and the Committee of Publishers Association and is legally binding throughout the United States.

Furthermore, the transmission, duplication or reproduction of any of the following work including specific information will be considered an illegal act irrespective of if it is done electronically or in print. This extends to creating a secondary or tertiary copy of the work or a recorded copy and is only allowed with express written consent from the Publisher. All additional right reserved.

The information in the following pages is broadly considered to be a truthful and accurate account of facts and as such any inattention, use or misuse of the information in question by the reader will render any resulting actions solely under their purview. There are no scenarios in which the publisher or the original author of this work can be in any fashion deemed liable for any hardship or damages that may befall them after undertaking information described herein.

Additionally, the information in the following pages is intended only for informational purposes and should thus be thought of as universal. As befitting its nature, it is presented without assurance regarding its prolonged validity or interim quality. Trademarks that are mentioned are done without written consent and can in no way be considered an endorsement from the trademark holder.

VIP Subscriber List

Dear Reader, If you would like to receive latest tips and tricks on internet marketing, exclusive strategies, upcoming books & promotions, and more, do subscribe to my mailing list in the link below! I will be giving away a free book that you can download right away as well after you subscribe to show my appreciation!

Here's the link: http://bit.do/jonathanswalker

CONTENTS

Part 1

Introduction

Chapter 1: Understanding Options Trading

Chapter 2: Risks And Benefits

Chapter 3: Strategies

Chapter 4: Keys To Success

Part 2

Chapter One: Investments With BlockChain

Chapter Two: Implementing BlockChain

Chapter Three: Smart Contacts

Chapter Four: Blockchain Pros And Cons

Part 3

Chapter 1: What Are Penny Stocks

Chapter 2: Picking The Right Trading Strategies

Chapter 3: Getting Started With Your First Trade

Chapter 4: The Basics of Investing

Chapter 5: The Different Investing Options

Chapter 6: The Best Investment Strategies

Part 4

Chapter 1 – Create An Ebook Empire

Chapter 2 – Create Killer Blogs

Chapter 3- Create Your Own Youtube Channel

Chapter 4 – Sell With Amazon FBA

Chapter 5 – Create Membership Sites

Conclusion

INTRODUCTION

Congratulations on purchasing this book and thank you for doing so.

The following chapters will discuss everything that you need to know about options trading. You will learn what options trading is, how to trade binary options, and the different strategies that you can use to get from zero to six figures, and more.

There are plenty of books on this subject on the market, thanks for choosing this one! Every effort was made to ensure it is full of as much useful information as possible, please enjoy!

CHAPTER 1: UNDERSTANDING OPTIONS TRADING

Options trading, also known as *binary options trading,* is just like forex and stock trading. However, you do not need to buy currencies or stocks. Instead, you simply predict whether the value of an underlying asset will increase or decrease at a specified time. It is this simplicity of options trading that attract so many investors. It is an option contract that has a fixed payout.

Options trading vs. forex and stock trading

In forex and stocking trading, you buy currencies or stocks and sell them for profit. In options trading, you do not need to buy any trading asset. You only predict whether the price of an underlying asset will be higher or lower than its current price at the expiration date. Also, in forex and stock trading, your profit will depend on the increase in the value of a particular currency or stock that you have purchased. In options trading, the potential profit is fixed and is revealed to you even before you commence a trade.

It is not uncommon for forex and stock traders to wait for weeks and months just to see a little profit from their investment. Many times, they even lose their investment without any chance of getting any profit. This happens when the price of their stocks or currency drops. With options trading, there is always a potential to earn a big amount of profit even when the price of an underlying asset decreases. You do not have to wait for weeks or months; you can double, or even triple, your investment in a few minutes.

Options trading vs. gambling

There are similarities between options trading and gambling. In some jurisdictions, options trading is literally considered gambling. Just like the casino game called *baccarat* where you decide whether the winning hand is *banker* or *player*, in options trading, you will decide whether the value of an underlying asset will rise (Call) or fall (Put) at the expiration time. Just like the table games in the casino, there is a fixed payout for a favorable outcome.

You might be wondering, "Is options trading gambling?" It depends. If you do options trading by relying on guesswork and pure luck, then you are gambling. However, if you consider every wager that you make an investment decision and take the serious effort to study the market and research the different underlying assets being traded, then you are an investor or trader.

It does not really matter whether you see yourself as a gambler or a trader. In the end, what matters is how much profit you have made, if any.

The Basics

Let us move on to the specific parts of options trading. Do not worry; options trading is very easy. You can learn the basics in less than five minutes. It is only like speculating the outcome of a coin flip.

Call vs. Put

There are only two main options to choose from. In options trading, you just have to know whether the outcome will be a *Call* or a *Put*. Simple, right?

Choose the Call option if you predict that the price of an underlying asset will be *above* its current price at the expiration date.

Choose the Put option if you predict that the price of an underlying asset will be *below* its current price at the expiration date.

These two terms are referred to by many names, depending on the trading platform that you use. They are also known as Up/Down, Above/Below, Rise/Fall, and others.

Strike price

This refers to the price at which an asset can be bought or sold at a certain time. In options trading, this simply refers to the Call or Put option. The Call option is the value at which the underlying asset can be bought, while the Put option is when it can be sold at a specified time.

Expiration time

The expiration time, or simply expiry time, signifies the end of a trading period. This is also the time when you can determine whether or not you have made the right investment decision. Therefore, this is the moment when you will experience a profit or a loss.

In-the-money vs. out-the-money

In-the-money is a *win*. It means that you have made

the right investment decision and earned a profit. On the contrary, out-the-money means that you have lost your wager.

Long-term option

In options trading, you get to choose how long a trade will last (expiration date). A long-term option simply refers to a trade that is long as 24 hours or more. A long-term option can last for a day, weeks, and months.

Speed option

As the name already implies, speed options are trades that last for a short period of time. This can be as fast as 30 seconds, a minute, or up to five to fifteen minutes, depending on the platform that you use.

Assets

Assets are valuable financial instruments. In options trading, you do not have to purchase any asset, you just have to determine if the value of an asset will be greater than or lower than its current price at the expiration time.

When trading binary options, the following assets are traded:

- stocks
- index
- commodities
- currency pairs

Bear market vs. bull market

On the one hand, a bear market means that the prices of certain assets are decreasing or are about to decrease. On the other hand, a bull market means that the prices of certain assets are increasing or are about to increase.

Take note, however, that even though a bear market is considered a negative sentiment, it does not affect you as a trader. In fact, you can even profit from it. This is because options trading has a dual nature: You can make a good amount of profit whether the price of certain underlying assets increase or decrease, provided you choose the right option (Call vs. Put).

Brokers and trading platforms

Before you can start trading binary options, you need to open an account with a broker. You can find many brokers when you make a search online. However, you need to choose a broker that will best suite your needs. Unfortunately, there are also scammers out there, so it is best to work only with a broker that has a well-established reputation.

Here is a list of trusted brokers. Take note that trading platforms may change their policies and management team. Therefore, even the most trusted brokers may no longer be a good choice tomorrow. Before you open an account, check the latest ratings and reviews given by other traders.

- iq option (www.iqoption.com)
- OptionRobot (www.optionrobot.com)
- Automated Binary (www.automatedbinary.com)
- Finpari (www.finpari.com)
- 24option (www.24option.com)
- fortuneJack (www.fortunejack.com) *bitcoin casino with binary options*

Important note:

Be sure to check the *banking options*. Many brokers accept many methods to make a deposit but only have limited options for making a withdrawal.

CHAPTER 2: RISKS & BENEFITS

Like any business venture, there are a number of risks and benefits associated with options trading. Here are the things that you can expect:

Market risk

The market is composed of real people. This is why it is extremely volatile. And, although there are methods that have been developed to predict market movements, there is no guaranteed way to determine how the market responds.

Lack of ownership

In options trading, you only wager on the future valuation of an underlying asset. Therefore, you do not exercise any right of ownership over any stock or asset.

High-risk investment

Like any other business that offers a high reward, the risk involved is also high. Unlike in trading stocks where you get to keep a losing stock with an opportunity that its price will soon increase or at least sell the stock to cut down your losses, you do not get to keep anything if you encounter a loss in options trading. In options trading, when you lose a trade, you lose the whole amount that you wager on that particular trade.

Limited opportunity

In options trading, the potential payout is already fixed even before you commence a trade. You cannot get a profit higher than the fixed payout. In forex or stock trading, the potential profit is almost limitless.

No liquidity

There is no liquidity because you do not have ownership of the stock or asset being traded. When you commence a trade, you just have to wait for the trading period to end and hope for the best. However, liquidity should not be an issue. After all, there are trades that can last for just a day, even less.

Losing is normal

Although there are people who rake in serious profits with options trading, the majority of traders lose their money, and they lose it within a short period of time.

If your entrepreneurial spirit remains strong and convinced despite the risks that you will encounter along your journey, then it is time for you to know the notable benefits of options trading.

The Benefits

High Return

For those who engage in forex or stock trading, a 50% is already considered high. And, usually, they would have to wait for months just to get a 50% profit. Most of the time, they do not even reach 50%. With options trading, getting a 90% per trade is normal. You can double your money in less than an hour.

Simplicity

It is the beautiful simplicity of options trading that makes it very attractive. You do not need to have any trading portfolio or any gambling experience. You can learn and start earning money with options trading almost instantly.

Fixed payout

Unlike other investment opportunities where you do not know how much money you can make, options trading lets you know the exact amount that you can profit before you commence a trade.

Quick turnover rate

Options trading allows you to choose just how long you want a trade to last. With speed trading, you can make multiple trades in less than five minutes.

Asset variety

Since you do not have to purchase any asset or currency, you have all the available underlying assets to choose from. Also, the minimum amount per trade is usually low, so you can easily diversify the assets that you invest in.

Controlled risk

You do not have to worry about hidden charges or surcharges. Whatever amount that you spend for a particular trade is your total risk. If you just want to risk $100, then simply invest $100, and there is nothing else that you should worry about.

Instant trading

Most established brokers offer a mobile phone feature. This will allow you to manage your account and commence a trade anytime and anywhere.

CHAPTER 3: STRATEGIES

Most people who lose their money with options trading either have no strategy at all and just rely on pure luck, or have a poor and underdeveloped strategy. If you want to rake in serious profits with options trading, you need to have a solid strategy. Unlike casino games where you simply have to vary the amount of your bets, success in options trading requires serious research, analysis, and practice.

Fundamental analysis

Fundamental analysis is considered the lifeblood of investment. This is the key to increasing your chances of making a profit. Remember that the market is run by real people and businesses, In fundamental analysis, you need to gather various information and analyze the economy, financial statements of businesses, as well as the latest news, among others. By analyzing these data, you can come up with a better investment decision. For example, if there is a report that the problem of the high unemployment rate has just been resolved in the U.S., and all other things being normal, then you can expect the value of the U.S. currency to increase.

If you like numbers, then fundamental analysis is the way to go. However, it is not recommended for speed options. This is because economic and business changes take time. It is best to use this method for trades that last for more than 12 hours.

Technical analysis

If you do not like analyzing lots of numbers, then technical analysis may be for you. Technical analysis is more visual. You will be analyzing charts and graphs. Technical analysis is excellent for fast trading or speed options. The proper way to use this method is to view the available graphs and look for patterns.

A note about patterns: Patterns depend on the latest trend. Is it a bull or a bear market? The risk here is that trends are not permanent. They change —and they usually change quickly. The key here is to find a pattern and be able to place your wager just before the trend changes.

Algorithmic and signals

By using computer programs and apps that can be installed on your computer, you will know where to invest in. This is an easy and quick way to come up with a decision; however, this method is not recommended because it is unreliable. There is simply no computer program that can accurately read the market's movement. However, this can be useful as secondary information.

Co-integration trading

This strategy uses the correlation that is created between two underlying assets. This usually occurs when two assets are in the same industry or have the same market. Due to their high correlation, you will notice that their prices are always close to each other. Hence, when a sudden significant gap appears between their prices, there is the highest probability that their prices will soon be close to each other again. So, you either place a Call option on the stock whose value has dropped or a Put option on the stock with a higher price.

Aggressive betting

As the name already implies, it is aggressive when you wager a big percentage of your total investment per trade, like wagering 20% per trade. Of course, the most aggressive way is to wager your whole investment on a single trade, but such is not recommended.

A famous aggressive betting strategy that is widely used by gamblers is known as the Martingale. This is where you double your wager after every loss. For example, first, you wager $10. If you lose the trade, you then wager $20. If you lose the trade again, you next wager $40, and so on... until you win a trade. When you win a trade, you go back to your initial wager of $10.

Although the Martingale looks feasible and reasonable, it is not effective in the long run.

Unfortunately, it is not surprising to experience a series of wrong investment decisions. If you get really unlucky, you may even make 10 wrong decisions in a row. There only use this strategy for a short term, and be sure to back it up with sufficient research.

Conservative betting

Your betting strategy is considered conservative if you only use a small percentage of your total investment per trade, preferably just around 1%-3%. This is good if you already have a well-developed strategy that has a high rate of success.

Corrective

This is a good strategy to use when you see a sudden and significant increase or decrease in price, especially when such price spike is not clearly justified by existing factors. In such a case, you can expect for the price to balance out by reverting to its original value prior to the price spike, or somewhat close to it.

Breakout

This strategy works well with currency pairs. When a currency pair follows a tight or close price difference, and if you see them break out, the probability is high that their prices will continue to breakout. Although they will most likely revert to their normal price range, such will take time.

Asset mastery

Pick any underlying asset of your choice. Now, find out everything that you can about your chosen asset. Follow on the news and gather as much data as you can about that asset. Do this on a regular basis, preferably daily. You will notice that the more you know about a particular asset, the better predictions you can make. This also confirms that the market does not move at random.

CHAPTER 4: KEYS TO SUCCESS

Regardless whether you only want to trade for profit or for fun, you should know the best practices that can help increase your chances of success and minimize your losses.

Money management

No matter how well developed your strategy is or how much you have increased your success rate, you can lose your investment if you fail to manage your money properly. Also, do not use the money that you need to cover your household bills and other obligations. Do not forget that options trading is a high-risk investment.

Cash out

An important part of money management is learning to cash out. Unfortunately, many traders do not cash out their profits. Although it is good to grow your funds, you should still cash out from time to time. Take note that your profits only become real when you turn them into real cash; otherwise, they are nothing but numbers on a screen and almost have no difference with demo credits. Therefore, always cash out, you do not have to cash out everything, if you want, you can just cash out 20% of your profits on a regular basis.

Research and analysis

The possibility of doing a research and analysis is what separates options trading from gambling. You need to research and be updated on the news about the businesses themselves, as well as the factors that affect business performance. When analyzing, you need to drop your personal preferences and see everything as they are. Your investment decision must be based on facts without any bias. Research is key. Remember that the outcome of every trade and the movements of the graphs are mere reflections of reality. The more you know about the economy, real people, and real businesses, the better you can make an investment decision.

Focus on the assets

Although the graphs and charts may reveal to you certain patterns, it is worth noting that such patterns are not always present. And, many times, they do not stay for so long. After all, trends are meant to change, considering that the market is alive and continues to move. When making an investment decision, be sure that you have good information on the asset that is the subject of your trade. It must be emphasized that the more you know about a particular asset, the higher is the probability of making the right investment decision.

The importance of keeping a journal

Although having a journal is not a requirement, writing a trading journal can be very helpful. You do not need to be a professional writer; you only need to be open and honest when you write your journal.

A journal will allow you to think outside the box and be a better trader. You can write anything in your journal. You can write about your new learnings, mistakes, or any adjustments that you make to your strategy. Should you decide to use a journal, be sure to update it regularly

Start small

It can be very tempting to invest a lot in a particular trade when you know that you have researched a great deal just to make that trade. However, if you are a beginner, it is best to start small and focus on increasing your success rate. First, you need to get a feel of options trading and develop your strategy. If it is your first time to trade, do not focus on making money right away. After all, once you have enough experience and confidence, you can easily increase the amount that you invest per trade. To have a good and steady profit, aim to have a success rate of at least 60%-70%.

Focus on the numbers

There are ways to somehow manipulate the stocks for a short period of time. Especially these days when you can easily and quickly send a message to the world with just a few clicks of a mouse, some people are able to make their stocks look more attractive than they really are. Unfortunately, even the media may have its own preferences and prejudices. And many so-called "experts" on options trading cannot be trusted. Therefore, you need to focus on the numbers. Words are easy to manipulate and misinterpret, but numbers do not lie. When numbers are unduly manipulated, such fraudulent scheme tends to be obvious.

Do not chase after your losses

When you engage in options trading, you should be prepared to encounter some losses. You cannot expect to make the right investment decisions all the time. Losses are part of this kind of investment. The important thing is that the outcome of all your trades results in a positive profit.

Never chase after your losses. If you do, there is a higher risk of losing more money. Instead, be positive and focus on your profits, and how to profit some more.

Most people chase after their losses by increasing the amount of their wager per trade. This is risky because your strategy may not be suited for an aggressive betting, and your funds may not be enough to handle such big wagers.

Develop your strategy

In options trading, developing a strategy simply does not end. This is because you are dealing with a living and continuously evolving market. Therefore, you should continuously work on your strategy. It must be flexible enough to adapt to market changes and effective enough to make a decent amount of profit.

Have your own understanding of the market

True experts do not have the same strategy or share the same viewpoints all the time. They are experts because they have developed their own understanding of the market, and they can justify their views no matter how odd they may be. In the same manner, you also need to develop your own understanding of options trading and the market. In the beginning, you can rely on expert tips and advice, but soon you need to have your own way of making an investment decision. After all, nobody can get rich just by relying on expert advice. Also, out of the many people out there who claim to be "experts," only a few of them are true experts. Most of these "experts" have more losses than profits.

Practice

The only way to truly learn options trading is by actual practice. It is experience that will make you a real binary options trader. Take note that practicing does not only mean making a series of trades. In options trading, placing a trade is the easiest part. True practice means doing research and studying the various underlying assets, businesses, as well as the market behavior, among others.

PART 2

Chapter one: Investments with Block Chain

The business models of several different companies in a wide range of sectors have been transformed by block chain. Looking at block chain, you are going to see that it appears to be a digital spreadsheet that is being worked on by members inside of an organization. The "digital spreadsheet" is going to be on a decentralized network.

Due to the way that block chain is written, it has some unique factors that are not going to be able to be understood, even by the investors that think that they can make a profit on that technology. Block chain is not like traditional trading because it has several different levels that are used.

Block chain offers at least five different ways that

you can make an investment that will benefit you later on.

1. Stockpile coins

Many investors are stockpiling gold so that they can wait to sell it whenever the price goes up sometime in the future. However, there are other investors that are stockpiling bitcoins. Stockpiling gold and stockpiling bitcoins are going to each have their advantages as well as their disadvantages but what it comes down to is the supply and demand. Whenever the supply is limited, the demand is going to go up, therefore, the value is going to increase which is going to be the opportune time to sell what it is that they are stockpiling.

2. Penny stocks

Penny stocks are a cryptocurrency like bitcoins just like Ether is a cryptocurrency, but they all work on a different system due to the fact that they are competing with bitcoin.

3. Crowdfunding with altcoin

Crowdfunding is a method that you can use whenever you are trying to raise capital for an investment. The coins are not going to need to be used when you are dealing with crowdfunding. Instead, people are going to give you coins before you start mining which is typically done before a system is opened to the public.

4. Angel funding and start up ventures

Block chain makes it possible for a great number of entrepreneurs and investors to come together and find each other to get funding.

5. Pure block chain technology

The technology behind block chain is on the rise, and the companies that are taking advantage of it are getting their name out there so that they can be better known whenever you find the block chain technology everywhere. A company by the name of Global Arena Holdings uses the block chain technology as leverage in getting their votes verified.

Chapter two: Implementing Block Chain

Knowing how you want to use block chain is vital before you get too deep into it. Block chain offers two ways to use their system, but ensure that you are choosing the one that is best for you. Typically people use block chain with an individual account.

With an individual account, you need to set up your wallet. Your wallet is going to be where you keep all of your bitcoins and will run off of most mobile devices and computers. Digital wallets are more secure than real wallets because they are not going to be stolen and they are most likely not going to be hacked.

When you use a software wallet, you are not going to be required to have a third party service for the wallet to be downloaded. Once it has been placed on your computer, you are going to have all of your transactions at your fingertips.

Next, you need to acquire bitcoins. You have the option to trade bitcoins for goods or services that you may be able to offer to those in the bitcoin system; however, it is hard to find someone who is willing to trade bitcoins because they do not want to give up their coins. You can also buy bitcoins in the marketplace where you can spend real world money and purchase as many coins as you want.

Lastly, you have the option to mine coins. Programs can be placed on your computer that will use a CPU that is customized to assist you in making a quick profit without you having to do many of anything.

You should make sure that your wallet is secured! Encrypt your wallet so that you are not leaving it open to hackers who want to steal your coins. If your coins are stolen, or bitcoin does not offer you an option where they will replace them because they are your responsibility.

Bitcoins can be spent just like regular money can be.

However, you need to find a merchant who will accept bitcoins as payment.

Chapter three: Smart Contracts

Smart contracts are probably going to be the aspect of block chain that will most likely be championed in the future. A smart contract is just a type of computer code that is activated once the block chain as a whole register that a predetermined incident has occurred. The smart contract is then given its own block and distributed as part of the chain.

While it may seem complicated, you can think of them in much the same way certain functions in a checking account work. In most checking accounts, automated deductions can be set up either by the user or by a third party with the user's permission. A smart contract works in broadly the same way but from a decentralized—not centralized--position. Put another way; a smart contract is the computer code equivalent of the legalese in a contract that stipulates how and when all the little details are carried out.

Additionally, as long as the smart contract is generated on a public block chain, then, unlike in the banking example, there is no third party (such as the bank) who is able to step in and actively prevent the transaction from occurring. The transaction is equally secure if it is performed by a bank or by a block chain. This is due to the extreme type of security that is built into the block chain model, the fact that the data is decentralized, and the extreme cost required to hijack a block chain.

What's more, unlike with traditional contracts, smart contracts that are executed via block chain are completely public and viewable by anyone with a copy of the chain. This means that the smart contract is never open for debate or discussion; it is purely an expression of the facts as they are truly stated. This can be seen as a miracle or a curse, of course, depending on the nature of the information being made public.

A smart contract is where a computer protocol can facilitate, verify, and even enforce the negotiation and performance of a contract in which the contractual clause becomes unnecessary.

The smart contract can also have a user interface that will emulate the logic of a contractual clause(s). The proponents of a smart contract claim that many different kinds of the contractual clauses may thus be made partial or even fully self-executing, self-enforcing, or possibly even both.

Smart contracts are going to aim to provide the security that is superior to any traditional law contract. This will, therefore, reduce the transaction costs that are associated with the process of drawing up a contract.

Common usage cases

With the rising market penetration of various financial technologies, smart contracts are becoming more and more prevalent. A big reason for that is because they are simplifying many common contract usage cases. For example, they are already making it easier for users to update various contract terms in real time, despite it taking days for physical copies to move back and forth to perform the same function. This not only improves the speed with which such processes can be performed but also greatly increases the odds of their accuracy remaining at acceptable levels throughout.

Smart contracts also activate automatically once certain real world conditions have been met, which means they require fewer resources to be utilized to the fullest. While this won't mean much to most users who use them infrequently, for business to business transactions, the savings will likely be substantial. The guaranteed and secure nature of a smart contract also means that it can be executed upon without the need for a third party to guarantee the transaction via escrow, reducing the closing costs of the contract on all sides.

Financial institutions will also find smart contracts useful in numerous ways. In regard to trade clearing or settlement scenarios, the final results relating to settlements, transfers, and trades is tallied automatically. Smart contracts can also be used when it comes to coupon payments, specifically to return principal on expired bonds. They also work with insurance claims as a means of minimizing errors and streamlining the flow of work between departments. Finally, they are also known to improve the regulation of Internet of Things services.

In the health care sector, smart contracts are known to offer up numerous advantages. For instance, they improve the accuracy with which medical records are updated as patients are transferred between departments. They can also be used to monitor the health of the population as a whole via public blockchains that update automatically and pay participants for using their information. Smart contracts are also already in use in many Internet of Things devices where they are used to determine the success of fitness goals and release rewards accordingly.

In the music industry, smart contracts are already being put to work tracking royalties for song usage and distributing payments accordingly. It is also being put to work on a smaller scale to enhance person to person interactions and is predicted to lead to things like trading energy credits and increased peer lending opportunities. This same technology is currently being adapted for use with the Tesla electric car, whereby users can charge at any charging station and be billed for the transaction automatically.

It is also changing the way large products are

shipped and tracked by sending out automated documentation as various production pieces make their way through processing, and on to shipping. This can even be cued to the input of certain signatures, meaning the process is seamless for signing the contract to receiving the goods. Later on down the line, if there are questions about the quality of the shipment, then the entire route the product took from creation to delivery can be tracked. This is due to the fact that it is on the same block chain that enables the creation of the contract in the first place.

For credit enforcement, the smart contracts are becoming an extension of property law. The credit agreements are going to disable the product that you have purchased if you fail to make the payments that you agreed to make. For example, if you buy a new car on credit and fail to make your payment. Then the doors to your car are going to lock and then drive itself back to the showroom.

However, most electrical products come with what is known as a kill switch that can be disabled should a condition not be met between the two parties. This would happen if the payments were being made through a public channel such as cryptocurrency.

Chapter four: Block Chain Pros and Cons

Block chain is not immune to have its pros and cons just like everything else that you can get involved in. While block chain is versatile, there are still those who are hesitant to switch over to the new technology when they can just stick to the methods they know work.

Block chain will protect your identity as well as work with you to make sure that your money is not stolen. Your personal information does not have to be entered into the block chain system in order for any transactions to be completed. It is going to be much like when you buy something with cash. You do not even have to enter a real email address. The block chain system gives you an email address, so that will change each time that you make a transaction on the system.

If there is any cost to send or receive a payment on the block chain system, it is not going to be a large fee. Any payments that go international will not force you to pay things such as transaction or exchange fees that a traditional financial institute would force you to do. Therefore, this will help keep all of your fees down when you find yourself traveling abroad.

One of the biggest cons that you are going to find with block chain is that you do not have the ability to reverse a transaction once you have made it. So, you need to be cautious when you are sending out coins because once it has been spent, there is a possibility that you are not going to get a refund from that person. Basically, keep a good handle on where you send your coins and have extra security on your system so that your coins cannot be stolen by a hacker.

Keeping your bitcoins means that you are going to have to deal with volatility. The value of bitcoins fluctuates with time and the longer you hold onto them, the less value they are going to hold when you are ready to spend them. So, you are going to be gambling with your coins and their value the longer that you hold onto them.

There are several companies such as Etsy and TigerDirect that are going to accept bitcoins as a form of payment rather than taking cash. However, big companies like Walmart and Target have not gotten on board yet, and there is no telling when they are going to get on board with bitcoin considering how well they are doing as it is. But, it is very likely that they are going to look into accepting bitcoins as the value of bitcoins goes up making it to where more and more people are using it.

Rather than being like a credit card, bitcoins are like cash. There are no extensions in the warranty that you have to deal with, but then again you are not going to have the rewards that you can get when it comes to using a credit card. Some places do not allow you to use a credit card for whatever policy reason that they have so then you are always going to worry about that as well. Then there are the fees and the added headache of if you do not pay it, it is going to affect your credit score.

Cash, on the other hand, is taken everywhere, there are no fees, in fact, there are many times that you end up getting a discount because you used cash. With bitcoin, you are going to be able to use it without the headache of late fees or other things that you are going to have to worry about with a credit card.

The biggest similarity that bitcoins has with credit cards is the fact that it is not going to be accepted everywhere.

On the business side of it, using bitcoin is going to save you money. If you are going to use services such as Coinbase, then the first million dollars that you make by accepting bitcoins is going to be free for you. It is from here that you are going to begin to pay at least one percent on all of the transactions that you do. However, this is still going to be considerably less than what you are paying in order to accept credit cards.

Exchanges that are doing with bitcoins can be converted easily without the need to worry about risking a lot of volatility. Not to mention, bitcoin eases any worries that you are going to have of chargebacks or even hackers getting into your system and stealing your customer's credit card numbers. The merchants that use bitcoin are normally going to work off of a tablet or even a smartphone when they are accepting a payment. This is an added benefit because you will not need a big fancy system that can only stay in one place. Therefore, you are going to be able to take your business with you anywhere and accept payments. Which is a major plus for your business!

PART 3

Part 1: Penny Stocks

Chapter 1: What are Penny Stocks?

Penny stocks are relatively simple, but there are a

few tricks that you need to learn in order to make them work for your needs. They represent stocks that are going to have a low price, usually a price that is under a dollar, as well as a smaller market cap that is under $500 million. For the most part, when an investor is working with penny stocks, they are going to be traded off of the traditional exchanges, so you will not find them on the New York Stock Exchange or on the NASDAQ.

So why would you want to choose to work with penny stocks rather than another investment type? There are several reasons to use penny stocks, but they are often used in order to help a company procure the right capital so that the company can grow and become more powerful. Through this market, the company is able to build up the money that is needed so they can grow their business and when you pick the right company, they can make a strong investment for a low cost.

Penny stocks are going to be traded in order to benefit some of the smaller public companies. But if this company does well, and you purchased the stock over the counter before it entered the regular stock exchanges, you could get a great return on investment. Even if the company never makes it over to the regular stock exchange, many of these can still increase their profits and you can earn back on your investment.

Almost all of the penny stocks are going to be sold on over the counter exchanges. This is going to work because many of the larger exchanges are going to have stringent policies before a company can join them and trade. Most of the companies that are in penny stocks will come nowhere near reaching these stringent requirements, plus it costs a lot of money to trade on these exchanges, so it isn't possible for some smaller companies to make it work. Instead of trying to meet some of these requirements or come up with large amounts of money that they don't have, the companies are going to work with the penny stocks to get the funding they need. As the investor, you are able to capitalize on this and get some great stocks, often from some growing companies, for a low price.

As the investor, you need to remember that there will be some risk that comes with going with penny stocks. If you take the time to educate yourself and learn how to avoid some of the major mistakes that come with this investment, you are more likely to make a good income in the process, but keep in mind there are some risks and they are sometimes seen as speculative in nature, rather than as an investment.

Benefits of going with penny stocks

First, let's take some time to look at the benefits of going with penny stocks. Penny stocks could be your next big break. They are a lot of fun to work with because there are a lot of companies who are out there and are looking to use penny stocks as a way to raise capital to grow and become big. If you pick out the right company, you could be one of the first people in on it, and that stock that you got for under a dollar will end up being worth a lot of money down the road if the company does grow.

That is one of the main benefits that come with investing is that there is the potential of making a huge return on investment. You need to make sure that you purchase a stock that is at a low price, which is easy to do in penny stocks, and make sure that it has a good business plan and will survive the market, just like you would with any other investment, and you will see results. Not all companies that are in penny stocks will make it to the big leagues, but many of them can still grow and you can make money from this process.

Many investors like to go with penny stocks because they are exciting and a lot of fun to work with. It is fun and can feel great, to start out with a little bit of money and then move up and see it grow. You may not make a ton of money at first, but penny stocks can help you to start with a small investment and get it to grow. If you want to start out your portfolio and you don't have a ton of money for it, penny stocks can be a great place to start.

The negatives of penny stocks

One of the first negatives that you should be aware of when you are working in penny stocks is that many of the companies on the market are not that good. There are some companies who are really good and just need to make a few tweaks or make a bit more profit before they are able to join the regular stock markets. But many of the companies that you will find in penny stocks didn't get onto the major stock exchanges because they were just bad. You need to learn how to tell the difference between the two if you would like to make an income here.

In addition, the penny stock market is not as reliable as the major stock markets. They are unreliable and they often don't have regulations in place to determine which companies or transactions that go on with them. This doesn't mean that all of the companies are bad on the penny stock market, but since there aren't really a lot of regulations that are in place, many bad companies can sneak through, make up numbers, or hide information and it is really risky picking out the company you want to work with. You will need to be diligent and really do your research to make sure that you are picking out good companies that will earn you money over time.

Penny stocks are really interesting investments to make. They usually have stocks that come in under a dollar each, so they are a good choice for those who have limited money to invest with in the beginning. While you do need to be on guard against some of the bad companies that are able to get onto the penny stock exchange, there are still many great ones that are available that you can pick from and that will help you to make a good return on your investment!

Chapter 2: Picking the Right Trading Strategies

When it comes to working in penny stocks, or any other investment for that matter, one of the most important things that you will need to do is figure out the strategy that you want to use. The strategy is so important because it is going to determine which stocks you will purchase when you will purchase them and sell them, and what research you will do to get the results. There are many great strategies that are available and none of them are necessarily any better or worse than the others, but you will find that picking a strategy and sticking with it, rather than bouncing back and forth between a few, can make all the difference. Some of the best trading strategies that you can use when you want to trade in penny stocks include:

Scalping

This is often a popular strategy to go with because it is pretty simple to use and many beginners like this simplicity. With the idea of scalp trading, you are going to take advantage of some of the inefficiencies that are going on in the market with respect to the spread. The gap between the bid price and the asking price, which is known as the spread, can end up widening or narrowing rapidly throughout time, and even through the day and they are going to create some great selling and buying opportunities that will result in some quick profits.

To scalp, you will need to be good at watching the market and understanding the perfect time to purchase and sale. You can even look at a few markets and see if you are able to find the stocks of a company a little lower than the price of them on the other. You would then purchase the stock at the lower price before moving it over to the other market and selling it for the higher price that is demanded there. You can end up selling the stocks pretty quickly this way and while the profit may only be a little bit on each one, if you purchase quite a few stocks and do this many times, you can make a good profit.

Range trading

When things are going along as normal and all of the other things in the market are even, stocks are often going to trade inside of a set trading range each day. When you use range trading to help you to purchase and sell your penny stocks, you will try to purchase the stock when it is at the bottom of the range, and then when it gets to the top, you will want to sell it. To do this type of trading, you will want to make sure that the stocks have a consistent trading range each day so that you can make some good estimates.

So with this one, you are going to take a look at some of the history of the company, if it is available, and find out what places seem to be the high points of the stock and which ones seem to be the low points. There can be some variations of this each day, but mostly you will notice that the trend stays about the same. You will then take this information to help you make the right purchases on all of your stocks. You will be able to make a purchase of the stock when the market is at the low end of the range and then you can sell the stock when it goes back up before it goes down and you lose out again. This one will require you to spend some time looking through many graphs and charts to get the information, but it can be pretty straightforward and can make you a good profit.

Momentum trading

This is the trading option that you will go with if you are looking to go with some of the trends that are in the market to make a good profit. In basic terms, you are going to use momentum trading or trend trading to purchase a stock when it is trending up, but then you will sell the stock as soon as the trend starts to go back down. This one can be a little less risky compared to some of the others, but you have to constantly be watching the trends and the market to make sure that you get out before all of your investment is gone.

Real-time new trading.

Another option that you are able to go with when

you are working on penny stocks is known as real time news trading. This is the one where you are going to have to spend some time reading or watching the news and looking for some clues as to how a market or a particular company is going to do. When you find that some good news is released, you will make the purchase, and then after that little punch up, you will sell the stock. It can also work to protect your investment because if you notice that some bad news is about to happen, you can sell the stocks without losing all the money, and then purchase them again when things settle down.

If you want to use this kind of trading strategy, you will want to make sure that you download a real-time news feed so that you are always getting information in. You also need to be able to understand what each piece of news can mean to the penny stocks that you are working with. You don't want to misunderstand what is going on and end up with selling a stock that was going up or losing out on a stock because you held onto it for too long.

When it comes to picking out the strategy that you want to use for your penny stocks, you will find that there is really no wrong answer. Each person is going to pick out a different strategy to help them out, and what works for one person is not going to work for you. Make sure to check out some of these strategies and then pick the one that works the best for you!

Chapter 3: Getting Started with Your First Trade

When you are ready to get started with your first trade in penny stocks, you will need to take a couple of steps. First, it is important to figure out the broker that you would like to work with. there are many different brokers available out there and many of them have great reputations that can help you to get done with your trading. You should compare a few of them right from the beginning, looking at the features that they offer, as well as some of the fees and costs that they will hand down to you. These will all affect how easy it is to do trades with your broker and how much you will actually make.

Once you have chosen the broker you want to work with, it is time to pick the strategy that you want to work with as well. There are many different strategies, and we discussed a few of them in the chapter above. These can all be successful based on what you would like to get out of the trading. The most important option here is to learn about the different trading strategies for penny stocks and then stick with it.

Many of the investors who end up failing are the ones who just can't seem to stick with the trading strategy that they originally picked. These are the people who will bounce back and forth between a few different options, but they never get familiar or comfortable with just one of them. You can pick any of the strategies that you would like, but you need to make sure that you are sticking with it if you want to see results.

Next on the list is to choose the stocks that you would like to invest in. This is the part that is going to take some time and you will probably need to use your chosen strategy to help you make the right decisions. When you are picking a stock to invest in, especially when it comes to the penny stock market, you want to make sure that you are being really careful. This is a fantastic market to get into, but if you are not paying attention and doing your research, you will find that your money will be all gone. Many good companies get onto the penny stock market, but so do many bad ones so you have to be diligent if you want to see success.

There are a number of things that you can do to make sure you pick out the right stocks when working in the penny stock market. First, make sure to check out the numbers on your own. Most companies want to gain your trust and will put up their sales information and other relevant things to help you make a good decision to go with them. But since this is not always required of stocks on the penny stock market, there are some that may not provide this information at all and some that will hide factors or fudge the numbers a bit. Doing your own research, and being critical to see if that research is correct, can be a great way to ensure that you are picking out good stocks that will help you earn money.

Always be critical when it comes to picking out a stock on this market. There are too many new investors who are excited to get into the trading business and who want to be able to pick out a company that will make it big. But if you jump in too quickly and don't pay attention to what you are doing while trading, you are going to end up in trouble, and probably losing a lot of money. Make smart decisions, pick out stocks that you think will do well, and always go through and do your own research, and you are sure to see the results.

And finally, after you have chosen your strategy and the stocks that you want to invest in, you have to decide how much you want to invest. Since the penny stock market is often inexpensive, with many of the options coming in at under a dollar, it is pretty affordable for you to make some purchase and get started. But even so, you will want to set the maximum that you want to spend on the stocks, as well as how much you are willing to lose before you get out of the market. Having this plan in place ahead of time can help you to make informed decisions, rather than ones attached to your emotions, and you will see much less risk in the process.

Along the way, if you happen to have any questions about how things are working or what you should do, turning to your broker can be a great idea. They have a lot of experience working in the various investments so they should be able to answer any of the questions or the concerns that come up and they can lead you in the right direction to making a good return on your investment.

Part 2: Investors Ultimate Guide from Novice to Expert

Chapter 4: The Basics of Investing

Many people are interested in investing, but they are not sure what steps to take to get started. Many times the information that is available can be confusing and once they enter the market, it is just too much to handle. Luckily, investing doesn't have to be hard, you just need to understand how to get started. Let's take a look at some of the basics that come with investing so that you can get started.

What is investing?

first, investing is going to refer to business activities where an investor will spend money in order to gain a profit. The investment is supposed to help the investor to make money and increase the value of their money through some business activities. There are many different ways that you can do this. You can choose to start your own business and invest funds into that, you can invest in the stock market, you can choose real estate investing, and so much more. But whatever type of investment that you choose, there needs to be at least some chance of making the money back and even making a profit, otherwise, it is too risky to work with.

All of the methods above are great ways to help invest your money, you simply need to pick the one that works the best for you. You should also spend some time learning how to reduce the risk of your investment. For example, if you wanted to start a business, you would learn about the market, make a good product, and find ways to sell the product so that you can make a good profit without losing out on all of your money. If you just go into an investment without some planning, you are basically gambling rather than investing.

Before you decide to get into an investment, it is a good idea have a little bit of savings ready to go. If you make smart decisions on your investment, you shouldn't have too many issues with losing all of your money, but some investments, such as real estate, can be labor and time intensive and having some savings in hand ahead of time can reduce the risk and help reduce the stress. Then when you start to invest, make sure that a few your profits go back into your savings to help out as well.

In addition, this savings can be a great way to get started on your investment. Most of us don't have a ton of extra money lying around that we can use for this kind of investment. But if we take a few months and put a little bit back for savings, it is easier to reach our goals. Then we are able to start investing without having to cut into our income or the money that we need to pay our bills when first starting out.

Before you are able to get into a new investment you need to pick out which one you would like to go with. There ae so many different options and part of the fun is figuring out which one is the right one to match up with your skills and interest levels. If you are interested in starting your own business, you can go with that investment, but other people may be interested in working in real estate and flipping houses or renting them out. Some people want to just invest their money with a friend or family member who is starting up something, and others like to work in the different parts of the stock market. All of these have the potential of being good investments, you just need to pick one and learn how it works!

Getting started in investing is a great way to make your money work for you. There are different options and all of them are going to require you to pick out different strategies to make them work. But when you are able to do this, you can make a good income from your investment.

Chapter 5: The Different Investing Options

So, in order to be successful with investing, you need to pick out the investment opportunity that works the best for you. There are a number of options that you can pick from, but as a beginner, you will probably want to start out with just one option. Yes, there are those investors who seem to have their hands in almost every market that is out there, but this can take some time to build up and as a beginner, that is going to be way too much for you to handle. If you are still considering which type of investment you want to work with and you aren't sure where to start, check out some of these options to help make the decision easier.

The stock market

The first place that people think about when they

are working on investments is the stock market. The stock market is basically a platform where shares of companies can be bought and also sold. The shares are going to be units of ownership in the company and when you purchase one of these shares, you become one of the owners of the company. Just like a traditional owner, you will be entitled to parts of the assets as well as the future profits of the company. So if the company grows and does well, you will make an income for holding onto the shares.

A common mistake with this is that new investors assume that they should purchase as many shares as they can to make a good profit. This can be one method to make a profit, but professional investors will agree that it is best to purchase stocks that have the potential to grow. You are going to make a bigger profit from 50 shares that go up to $100 each compared to 100 shares that go up to $2 each, even if you ended up purchasing them for the same total price.

There are many options when it comes to investing in the stock market. Some people choose to pick a company to invest in for the long-term and will hold onto the stock, earning a profit each quarter as long as the company does well. Day trading is popular as well and it includes you purchasing and selling the stock all on the same day to make a bunch of little profits that add up. You can also choose from forex trading, options trading, and penny stocks as well. Each of these have their own unique set of rules and own risks so make sure that you fully understand them before starting.

The bond market

Another investment type is to work with the bond market. With this option, you are taking on less risk and you know right from the beginning how much you will earn in interest, but the return on investment is lower than the stock market or other options. In the bond market, the government and other companies are looking to borrow money from investors to expand their business or to do other things to help them grow. The investor will be able to lend out this money in the form of a band, and the company or the government can then use it for their plans.

With the bond, you will invest a certain amount of money that you are not allowed to take out again until the maturity date of the bond. Sometimes this will be a few months but it can go for several years. You will get to determine the maturity date that you are comfortable with before you start. The bond will have an interest rate attached to it, which is the amount that the investor will earn on their investment when the maturity date hits. It is a safe and secure way to make a little bit of money on your investment and can help you to grow your portfolio without all the risk that is found with some of the other options.

Investing in commodities

Some investors like to invest in commodities to see a profit. Commodities are going to refer to produce that is high in demand and also publicly traded. The products themselves will not be traded on this market. The speculators and the investors in this market are going to contract for the future value of the product. Let's look at an example of coffee. Many countries will produce coffee and this can be a great commodity to work with.

With this system, you are going to pick the commodity that you want to work with and then sign a future contract for the amount that you will spend, say $100,000. If the price of the coffee goes up by the end date, you will be able to get a profit. But if for some reason the price of the coffee goes down, you will lose the money. You need to have a good idea of the market for the commodity that you want to work with and be able to estimate what is going to happen with it in the future in order to make money with this option.

Foreign exchange

Working with foreign currencies is another option that is available for a trader. With this option, you are going to make a purchase of another currency, perhaps the GBP, when the price is relatively low compared to the American one. Then you will wait until it is worth more in the future, and change it back over to the USD, making a profit in the process. For example, if you changed over to the GBP when it was worth $1.2 USD, and then held onto it for a bit until 1 GBP was worth $1.5 USD, you would make a profit of $0.30 on every dollar that you spent, which can add up if you did a larger investment.

This was traditionally a method that was only used by the banks and governments of different countries, but it is now an option that many different people are able to use thanks to the newer technology. You do need to be careful with this option though because the currency market is always fluctuating and you never know if your money is going to be worth more or less in the future. But if you are able to hold onto the money for some time and can watch the exchange rates, you can make a good profit from this option.

Starting your own business

Some people choose to start their own business in order to start a new investment. There are many options that you can choose, from brick and mortar stores to working from home. But no matter what kind of business you decide to start, you will have to put some money forward to get started. For example, even if you want to be a writer from home, you will need to invest in a good computer, some writing software, the internet, and even some storage to help keep files in order. If you want to start a clothing store, you would need to rent out a building, purchase the clothes, hire employees, and so on.

There is quite a bit of risk that can happen with starting a business, but if you think it all out, come up with a good business plan and stick with it, you can start to make a good profit from your own business. Plus, you are able to work for yourself, instead of being stuck with a boss, so it can be very appealing to many people.

The real estate market

Many people like to work with the real estate market because this is a market that is often going up. There are some different options that you are able to use when it comes to working in the real estate market, which can make this even more popular since you get to choose the one that works for you. One option that works well with real estate is flipping houses. With this option, you will purchase a home when it is really low in price, perhaps as a foreclosure or when the market is really low. Then you will make some changes to the home, fix it up and make it look nice, and then when the market starts to go up, or when the value is higher, you will sell it to make a profit.

If you are looking to get a more continuous form of income from real estate, you can choose to purchase a home and rent it out. Your rental fees should be enough to cover the cost of the home (or the mortgage) as well as the taxes, maintenance and for you to make a little bit of income. Over time, you can add in a few different properties so that you can make a full-time income in the process.

In addition, there are a lot of options that fall into

the different categories. For example, working with rentals can include single family homes, duplexes, and apartment buildings and you can even work with commercial real estate as well. It all depends on the amount of work that you would like to put into the investment and how much money that you would like to earn.

As you can see, there are quite a few different options that you can pick from when it comes to working on an investment. All of these have the potential to bring you a lot of income, but you just need to pick out the one that meets your interests and that you will enjoy doing the most. Pick out your investment, and you are sure to see a great income in no time!

Chapter 6: The Best Investment Strategies

The next thing that you need to focus on, after you have been able to pick what kind of investment that you would like to work on, is to pick a good strategy that will help you to get this all going. There are a lot of investment types and all of them are going to work in a slightly different manner, so once you pick the investment option, you will need to look a bit more in depth to see what strategies are the most effective for you. But no matter what kind of investment you go with, there are a few strategies that will work for all of them including.

Buy low and sell high

In all of the investments that you work with, the goal is to purchase your asset at the lowest price that you can. If you purchase the investment at a price that is too high, you are going to lose out or not make very much money in the process. You are going to need to work on learning the market in order to understand when is the best time to make the purchase.

When it comes to the stock market, you will want to wait for the market to go down a bit, or at least a dip in the company that you are working with. This will allow you to purchase the stock at a lower price than usual, and then you just need to hold onto the stocks for a bit of time until the market goes up. Of course, you need to learn the difference between a stock being low priced because of the market and it being low priced because the company is failing.

You can use this in other investments as well. When it comes to working with real estate, you will want to look for a downturn in the housing market to get a good discount on the homes you want to purchase and then wait until the market goes back up and you can sell the home for a much higher price. The good news with real estate is that you can rent out the home, and make some income in the process, while you wait for the market to go back up.

No matter what kind of market you get into, you must make sure that you are purchasing the asset at the lowest price possible. This will ensure that your risks are lower and your profits higher. If you aren't good at reading the market and working on your strategy, you will find that you will purchase the asset at a high price and that it will be very difficult to sell it again without taking a loss. The lower that you can get the asset, without picking one that is already failing, the better off you will be when it comes to making a profit.

Be an expert in your market

The idea behind this strategy is that you stay inside just a few markets. You may look at the list of investing options above and feel that you should jump into all of them, but when you generalize in everything, you are setting yourself up for failure. As a beginner, you need to just stick with one option. This allows you to devote your time and energy to this, without becoming overwhelmed. Over time, as you become an expert in that market, you can expand out a little bit and try a few other options, but you should really just concentrate on one at a time and even when you expand, keep the markets similar.

For example, if you want to go into real estate, you

should consider working first in renting out single family homes. Do that for a bit of time until you become comfortable with what you are doing and then you can consider expanding your portfolio to not only rent out these single-family homes but to also expand out to renting out duplexes and some small apartment buildings. You are still within the same field, but you are growing your income and diversifying your portfolio all at the same time.

If you are working in the stock market, you can take kind of the same approach. You may start out with a long-term investment in a few stocks, but then over time, you may decide to add some Forex trading or some penny stocks to the mix to help diversify and make more money. You are still working in the stock market, or something similar to it though, so you can take your knowledge and expand it out to other investments.

The thing that you need to watch out for with these

investments is skipping from one to another. If you have been doing real estate, you may find that it is hard to jump over to the stock market and going from the stock market to the real estate market can be tough as well, because they are really two different types of investments. Some people have been able to do it, but it is tough and you may find that it is too much to put onto your plate. It is better to just stick with the one market, become an expert in it, and then diversify within it to see the profits that you want.

Pick out financial safe havens

After you learn a bit about how to invest into the stock market or another market for investing, you may want to learn a bit about financial safe havens. These are places where you are able to transfer your money during an economic downturn and which are less likely to be negatively impacted by the market. You would put your money over to these in order to avoid losses, at least until the economy comes back around. Ideally, your safe haven is going to be able to at least beat off inflation so you will still have the same spending power later on.

There are several different types of instruments that you can use for this, but gold is one of the most popular ones. Big investors will often move their money over to gold when the economy gets tough, and this is why you will see that the price of gold will start to climb when markets like stocks and bonds start to do poorly. Gold is not the only safe haven that you can pick. In bearish markets also see a rise in treasury bills, but gold is still the most popular because the interest rates are so low on these treasury bills.

Invest actively

If you are able to get started with a larger sum of money, you are able to start investing in an active manner in the market that you choose. In order to use this particular strategy, you must learn how to become an expert in the chosen industry and focus your energy on these in order to better learn these markets and to make some of the best decisions possible to grow your money.

For example, if you are using this type of strategy, you may want to spend some time reading up on the news of any company that you are interested in investing with. In addition, you would take some time to look at the financial statements of the company, check into their management, and find out if they are growing consistently and are actually a company that you want to work with.

There are thousands of companies who are on the stock exchange and it is important that you learn how to be an active investor. Sure, you could hand over the money to a broker and hope things go well, but the most successful investors are the ones who do the research and pick out the strategy that they want to use on their own. There is nothing wrong with talking to a broker and getting some advice, but you should never let them do all of the work for you.

Focus on the goals

Before you enter into any of the investment types, you should sit down and have some clear cut goals. You want to have a purpose behind your investing and what you want to do if you are actually successful. This will help you to create a system that will lead you to meet this goal. Some people will invest in order to make some side money to help them out with bills and other things, some want to put that money towards retirement and to help them build up a little nest egg. Others are tired of working a regular job and want to be able to work for themselves. Having these goals will help you to see that success, no matter what it is.

For example, if you are looking to make this into an investment into your retirement, you may be more likely to look for long-term investment opportunities that will help you to earn a little bit over each month. If you want to make this into a full-time income, you are going to be more interested in things like flipping homes or riding some of the big waves of the stock market so you can make this income. As you can see, these are very different options of investing, but it always depends on the goals that you are trying to reach for which one you will choose.

So before you decide to go and purchase your asset or get into your chosen market, you need to sit down and decide what your goals are going to be for that investment. Then you can write down the plan that you want to follow in order to make these goals a reality. It is nice to have dreams and to hope that the investment asset that you choose will help you to get there, but if you don't plan ahead and make sure that you have the right strategy, you are never going to see the results that you want.

It is so much you are able to do when it comes to picking out an investment and seeing it grow. Picking out a good strategy will help you to really see the success that you are looking for because it leads you to pick the right asset and making decisions that will make you successful. No matter what kind of investment you choose to go with, make sure to follow some of these simple strategies and you are sure to see some of the success that you are looking for.

PART 4

INTRODUCTION

Haven't you heard every successful internet entrepreneur worth his courses and blogs talk obsessively about passive income? Their focus is always on creating solid, multiple and life-long streams of wealth. So, what exactly is passive income? Why is it such a buzzword among online marketers? Why is everyone scurrying to harness the power of the internet to create income streams that last forever?

We've all been a part of the daily grind that trades time for money. We trade specific numbers of hours and get paid for only those many hours. And there's a perpetual financial crunch when it comes to meeting our expenses. To fill the gap, we take on part-time jobs, work overtime, work weekends and unfortunately, it is still not enough. We are still trading time for money. There are but 24 hours in a day, and there's only so much we can make if our income is equivalent to the time and effort we put in a day. How then does one experience exponential growth in income without spending a fortune? How does one always have enough money to enjoy the good things life without slogging night and day? Passive income is the key.

Notice how some people have all the time in the world but no money to enjoy the time at hand, while others have all the money they need but no time to enjoy the money since they are busy using that time to make money. Passive income gives you both. The time to enjoy the money you earn and the money to enjoy the time at hand. Unfortunately, a majority of the folks are so caught up in the concept of financial security that they sacrifice their financial freedom for it. True financial freedom comes when you have both time and money to enjoy your life without thinking about where the money for your next bill will come from.

As life progresses, you realize that you've traded financial freedom for financial security, where your time, income and efforts are controlled by someone else. You realize that you've been a bucket carrier all your life who goes to work on a particular day, works according to the dictates of others and then brings home a bucket of water (income). Contrast this with passive income, which is more like building a pipeline of wealth. When you create a pipeline of capital, the water automatically flows from the tap whenever you want it to. You don't have to go out and put in hours of hard work and time to get the water home in a bucket. When you create powerful, practical and multiple sources of income - the income simply comes gushing to your house. It isn't a natural process of course, but nothing in life that's worth having is ever easy. It may take days or months to create a pipeline, but it is a one-time effort that can give you a lifelong source of income. To quote an oft repeated internet marketing cliché which is indeed true, with the passive income you literally make money while you are sleeping. Or holidaying in the Alps. Or attending your child's school function. You do not have to work large numbers of hours to rake in a substantial income.

Now there are many ways to earn passive income. You may think of owning real estate and leasing it out as a form of passive income. Then some investments can give you a sound passive income based on the interests these investments generate. However, think about the upfront investments these sources of income require. Purchasing pricey real estate or setting aside a huge sum for investment purposes is no mean feat. You may make a decent amount of passive income in return, but the investment may just not make it worth it.

Let us look at online passive income streams now. They require minimal investment and can help you witness exponential financial growth. Other than a low investment, all you need is time and information to get started, and you may well be on your way to creating a treasure house of income. Most well-known online entrepreneurs didn't start as millionaires. They barely had enough money to pay their bills and sustain. They were just perceptive, tenacious and resourceful enough to channelize the power of the internet to create smart income streams. There's no reason why you cannot do the same.

This book has just about everything you need to know about building passive income streams online. I have tried my best to share the little-known strategies and proven secret sauce that differentiates average internet marketers from the really successful ones. There are lots of actionable points and nuggets of wisdom that can help you build strong, diverse sources of passive income online with little investment. You will learn how to think out of the box and become an innovative online entrepreneur. More than anything – you will discover the joy and gratification of creating sources of wealth that give you greater freedom. Think –the freedom to spend time with your loved ones, the freedom to live life on your terms and the freedom to work for your profits rather than the net profits of a corporation. Get on the passive income lane now and enjoy the ride!

Chapter 1: Create an eBook Empire

Well yes, the truth is - people are loving eBooks. A comprehensive 2012 survey by Pew Research Center discovered that about 43 percent of Americans read a book or long content (journals, magazines, etc.) on an electronic device. The survey also revealed about 28 percent Americans owned a minimum of one electronic reading device. You can only imagine how much the numbers would have grown since. Packed with practicality (well, even the biggest home library may not be able to accommodate a million books), portability and quick access, eBooks are transforming the way people read. Why not cash in on this wonderful development and create some useful, information-packed and exciting books that will add value to people's lives? Here's all the meat and juice for creating your own successful eBook empire.

Find a Passion

We all have that one thing which lights the fire in us. What is that one topic or niche which you can talk on or write about for hours? Fitness? Psychic powers? Cooking? Raising children? Write down a list of possible ideas you can think of which you see yourself writing with knowledge and passion. Build mind maps once you've decided on the core topic. These can include all the sub-topics you may want to include within the main subject. For instance, if you are putting together a fitness related eBook, think of all the chapters/sub-topics/sub niches to be included in it.

This can be fitness workouts, diets to complement your workouts, ideal fitness attire, fitness gear, fitness stretches and the likes. Similarly, if you find the marketplace is already crowded with too many fitness related books, you can narrow down your focus to a single aspect of fitness. Say Post Pregnancy Fitness – How to Get Back in Shape After Having a Baby. If you are already an expert in a particular niche, such as a child psychologist or real estate attorney or wedding planner, jump right in within your area of expertise.

Start Writing

Once you have a topic in place, begin a rough table of contents draft for the book. This will help you flesh out the topics later. You can use any word processor such as Notepad or Word. Some people prefer Evernote. If you are not comfortable writing it as a single document, break down the documents chapter-wise. This way you can move around and access various chapters quickly and then put them together in the end.

You will have to play around with images, font sizes, colors and headers to make huge chunks of text easy to read. Make the book look attractive, easy on the eye and navigation friendly. In the end, put all the chapters together to create a seamless flow.

Convert It into an eBook

A simple Google search should give you multiple options for converting a word document into an eBook. You simply need to upload a Word file, and it is transformed into an eBook. A calibre is a free software that can be downloaded and used for word processor to eBook conversion. Go through everything to ensure the formatting is in place. If you are using Amazon Kindle Publishing (inarguably the best platform for eBook greenhorns), there's a preview tool that lets you see a final version of the book, so you know exactly how the formatting will appear on electronic devices.

Create A Stunning Cover

You can create a gorgeous looking eBook cover using either some type of graphic software program such as Photoshop or Ms. Office (Powerpoint, Word, etc.). You can also hire the services of expert graphic designers on freelance project sites. Look at other covers for inspiration. Get a feel of them on the Kindle eBook store. Once you have a design and layout in mind, create and upload it. Amazon also has a handy cover creator, which can be used for building quick and effective eBook covers. Amazon will only display your book cover in the "Customers Who Bought This Item Also Bought" to trigger reader curiosity. Ensure that it is sharp, attention-grabbing and relevant.

Pricing Your eBook

Amazon gives you the option of picking your own book pricing plan. You can either avail 35 percent profits by setting your own price or 70 percent profits by pricing your book according to Amazon's prescribed price between $2.99 to $9.99. Unless there is a strong business plan behind pricing your book outside $2.99 to$ 9.99, it makes sense to keep a significant chunk of your profits.

Promote The Book Extensively

Amazon will only boost your sale and reach when you fulfill the requirement of their sophisticated algorithms. You will have to promote and push your book initially to get support from them. This can be done by creating a few high-quality guest blog posts on sites/blogs related to your book. You can include a snippet about the book in the author bio to pique the interest of readers. Another great way is to take interesting and meaningful lines from your book and convert them into quote memes or tweets. Lots of people sharing and re-tweeting them will help you garner a large audience. Include a link to your book wherever permissible. Social media updates, blogs, email signatures and the likes.

A good way to build a bank of reviews and customers is to distribute free copies to people within your social network and ask them for genuine reviews. You can also price the book at a discounted rate in the early launch stages and ask the first few buyers to write reviews, before changing to the regular price. It always helps to have some reviews in there when readers are trying to make purchase related choices.

Another advantage of having a lot of early buyers is that Amazon boosts popular titles and gives it, even more, exposure once they see a lot of people picking it up. This can massively help your rankings.

Other Publishing Channels

Other than Kindle Publishing, you can also publish your book on your own website. It may not enjoy a roaring exposure initially or at least not as much as a large platform like Amazon, however over a period of time; you can enjoy higher profits. Third party hosting merchants may charge you a small percentage fee of about 1 to 5 percent for accepting customer payments and delivering the content to them in a downloadable format.

Chapter 2: Creating Killer Blogs

Blog- the internet marketer's golden word. And rightly so. Imagine creating a single valuable, detailed, comprehensive and well-researched post just once and earning from it years after you have published it. Blogs can be used in tandem with other passive income sources such as membership-based training programs or eBooks. They can also be stand-alone income generators. You can earn revenue through advertising programs such as Google Adsense. Then there's the highly lucrative world of affiliate marketing and list building. Selling banner advertisements, physical products, courses, eBooks and more is just the tip of the iceberg. There is really so much you can do with an informative, valuable and content-packed blog.

Pack Value Which is Tough To Find Elsewhere

Pick a topic you are passionate about and know well. Do not incredible trend hop and know what topics are popular. Yes, you need to do basic keyword research to determine if there's sufficient demand for your niche but don't obsess too much about finding the most populated niches. The challenge is to grab any niche you like and make it popular! Go with specific topics or sub niches to laser target your audience and gain monopoly within the sub-niche. For instance, if you find that weight loss is an overcrowded niche, try dominating a sub-niche such as a post pregnancy weight loss or weight loss for seniors. This way you get a more focused audience who you can sell and market to with comparatively lesser competition.

Create Interesting and Valuable Content

Create original, engaging, unique and useful content that gives your readers more value. Explore your expertise and write about something that you have a sound knowledge or background of. Use powerful elements to support your text such as images, videos, and infographics. Use screenshots wherever required to make the content clearer for your target audience. This will require more time and effort than a simple text blog. However, it will help your search engine rankings and will give you lots of loyal readers.

Choose A Blogging Platform

If you are serious about starting a blog that generates passive income, avoid using a free blogging platform and opt for the WordPress self-hosted medium. WordPress is one of the most widely used, customizable, easy to operate and visually stunning blogging platforms. The self-hosted option allows you to set up banner advertisements and use affiliate market links within the blog. Your blog URL looks more professional, in addition to the fact that you will be able to play with abundant features for beautifying your blog. Find a reliable hosting service and a brandable, memorable and unique domain name.

Blog Interface

If content is the king, your blog design is the queen. It will determine many factors such as the stickiness of your blog, the time people spend on your blog, the click through rate of your links and much more. Opt for a clean, well-defined and user-friendly interface. Use can either use a WordPress theme or buy them from a third party like Themeforest.net. You can also pick between free and paid themes. Paid themes add more bells and whistles to your blog to make it look attention grabbing and professional. Themes can be changed instantly by going to the Appearances section of your WordPress admin panel. Ensure you pick a responsive theme for your blog as a majority of users access the Internet from handheld devices.

Make it easy for visitors to find everything on your blog by organizing all relevant tabs on your home page. Balance colors well, and leave enough white space to give the eye some relief. Use customized headers created by a professional graphic artist. Improve the readability of your blog by using subheads, bullets, text bubbles for critical text, tables, charts, illustrations and more. This helps attention starved people pick key points from your content without having to go through the entire piece.

Monetizing The Blog

Advertising Program – You can 'rent' out space on your site to popular advertising programs such as Google Adsense, Yahoo Bing Network, Clicksor and more. These ad networks keep the advertisements relevant to your blog content and pay you a small amount every time a visitor on your site clicks on the advertisement. The best part is you aren't creating or selling any products but merely using the space on your blog to create passive income.

Affiliate Marketing – Affiliate marketing is all about selling other people's products on your site and earning a commission on every sale or lead that is fulfilled through a link on your blog. Say for instance, you run a pet travel site and have a steady stream of pet owners who travel with their pets. You can sign up as an affiliate for a puppy discipline informational eBook or a nationwide network of pet care and grooming services. So each time a pet owner buys the book or signs up for the pet grooming services, you get a nice little commission. Though individual products and services may have their own affiliate program, some popular marketplaces where you can find several affiliate programs are Clickbank, Offervault, Markethealth, ShareASale, Commission Junction and Avangate.

1. Review Writing – Writing useful, comprehensive and well-researched reviews is one of the best ways to sink your teeth into the world of affiliate marketing. Identify high-quality products with top-notch customer support, which can be really useful for your audience. Draft lengthy reviews to promote the products (include both pros and cons) and make your buyer's decision making process simpler. Reviews are often sought by people who are already half way within the buying cycle (with some options at hand) and giving them a good overview of the product will help you complete the sale.

2. Promote The Right Products – This should be fairly obvious yet it is surprising how many folks get it all wrong when it comes to promoting the right products. Find products that feature high ratings, superior quality, decent recommendations and most important – are relevant for your audience. Promoting dubious products and scams spell doom for affiliate marketers. You might make those first few sales by luring people, however your long term credibility may take a massive blow. If you plan to stick around for long and build a dependable source of passive income, pick your products judiciously.

3. Think Out Of The Box – If you believe the virtual world is already choc-a-bloc with multiple affiliate offers, think out of the box and act as an affiliate for local businesses. Use conventional businesses to generate profitable commissions. For example, let us assume you run an interior design and decorator blog that gives people interesting home makeover

ideas. You can tie up with home improvement companies, contractors and furniture suppliers in your neighborhood for lead capturing or selling their products to your readers. You may also be running a city or region based blog, and promoting local businesses may be the perfect passive income business model.

4. Diversify – Diversify your affiliate marketing offers, yet do not crowd your blog with too many sales pitches. Pick a handful of good offers and start promoting them. For example, for a travel blog, you can promote multiple products/programs such as backpacks, a traveler blogger training program, photography equipment and more. This way you are catering to diverse needs and pulling in bigger profits.

5. Links – Use link cloakers to get rid of the ugly, long and unprofessional looking affiliate links. They make your links appear cleaner, shorter and more

professional, while also boosting your click-through figures. Another pro tip is to make the visuals on your blog clickable. When images are made clickable by linking back to the sales page of the offer you are promoting, enthusiastic customers are immediately led to the relevant buying page. When you are eagerly looking to buy something or thinking about buying something, you don't want a tacky looking image upload page to play mood killer. User experience is a huge factor in determining the success of your affiliate marketing blog.

6. Selling Banner Ads – Once your blog attains considerable popularity, you can consider selling banner ad spaces to businesses related to your blog. You have complete control over how much you charge these firms since you are directly dealing with them. If you draw impressive traffic figures from a well-targeted audience, companies will be willing to negotiate lucrative advertising revenue.

7. Selling Informational Products – Selling your own digital products is another source of passive income. These can eBooks, short reports, email courses or membership programs. If you have high-quality, original and problem-solving content on your blogs, you will build a loyal base of readers who trust your expertise. They will be more than happy to buy informational products from you. The book can be sold to your mail subscribers or directly on your blog/website using an attention-grabbing landing page. You can also put the book for sale on the Amazon Kindle Publishing platform.

8. Directory Listings – When your blog becomes somewhat popular, you can start a paid listings section and rake in a good amount of income from it. The services can be related to your blog content. For instance, if you are running a blog related to wedding planning, and pull in a massive traffic of soon to be brides, you can put up listings of

professionals offering wedding related services such as florists, bakers, decorators, jewelers and travel companies. This helps to add an extra income avenue to your blog. Passive income is all about diversifying and optimizing revenue from a single source.

9. Pay Per Lead For Local Businesses – Imagine you have a thriving blog that focuses on real estate and attracts lots of real estate buyers and sellers who are hungry for information. How about working out an arrangement with local real estate firms/professionals to pay you per buyer/seller lead you send them? Leads can be captured by informing your audience that you can help them find some of the best properties in their area. It is a win-win situation for all. Again, passive income is thinking out of the box and leveraging multiple income streams to maximize your profits.

10. Promotions and Paid Recommendations/Reviews

- Once you gain considerable authority in your niche and are often referred to as an industry influencer, you can easily do paid reviews/recommendations or draft promotional posts. At this stage, you will most likely have a large following of people who trust your opinion. Cash in on it by promoting others' products and services through promotional posts. Make sure that you don't fill your blog solely with promotional posts and maintain a delicate balance between promotional and non-promotional content. The idea is not merely to sell to your target audience, but to help them buy by recommending really great stuff which makes their life simpler.

11. List Building - A blog that attracts a steady stream of targeted visitors can be great for list building. Place a sign-up box prominently on your blog to attract a swarm of organic subscribers from well-targeted traffic. These are a bunch of already interested action takers, and you could sell just

about any related offers, programs, courses, services and products to them. When people sign up for a mailing list, they are voluntarily expressing their interest in knowing more about the products/services being promoted by you. These leads can be used to generate a decent amount of passive income by boosting your sales conversions.

To get potential customers to sign up for your list, make them an offer they can't refuse. Throw in a free eBook or offer them a 10-15 day course. You can also include your affiliate links within the eBook or course. For example, if you are offering an eBook that offers WordPress site creation to beginners, you may want to suggest a good domain name registration and hosting service. Sign up as an affiliate of a reputed web hosting and domain name service and recommend it to your buyers in the course of the book.

Chapter 3: Create Your Own YouTube Channel

Did you know that YouTube has 60 hours of video uploaded to it every 60 seconds? Or that more than 4 billion videos are watched every day? The platform gets a crazy 800 million unique visitors every month (source – Jeffbullas.com). There is a marked shift from consuming text related content to content that is more interactive and real time. Users with small attention spans find it way more convenient to see something than reading about it. Also, the demand for video-based content is at an all-time high, with lesser competition than text-based blogs. Not many people are confident about facing the camera, and that's where you can cash in while space is relatively less crowded.

Belonging To The Big G Family Helps

Since YouTube comes from the Google stable, it is hugely favored by the big G in their organic search results. If you optimize your video for search engines by using the right keywords in the title, meta tags, and descriptions, your videos will enjoy higher placement rankings in search results. It is much easier to get a YouTube video to rank on Google compared to a blog post.

Go With Technical and Problem Solving Topics

The nature of YouTube fits very well with technical and problem-solving topics where people are looking for very specific solutions. For instance, someone may want to know how to create a table of contents in MS Word or the basics of using MS Excel. Isn't it easier to get a step by step demonstration of using these features rather than only reading about them? Similarly, cooking, DIY crafts, and product demonstrations are extremely popular on YouTube.

When users watch videos on your YouTube channel, there are related ads that pop up on the screen. When visitors click on these ads, you get paid for it. This is why it is emphasized that you have a focused and clear problem-solving niche. Comedians or other YouTube performers may not enjoy much ad relevancy since they do not have a very targeted audience. However, if you are extremely popular, you may make a considerable income even with low click through rates.

Unconventional ways to approach a common topic works wonderfully on YouTube. Throw in a lot of wit, creativity, visual play and humor to illustrate complex topics. Offer interesting metaphors and analogies, and include surprise elements that make your audience take notice.

Use Your Watermark For Videos

Always use a watermark of your blog for your videos. This way users will know exactly where the videos originated from, which will make it easier for them to track your blog and channel. Some users may embed your video on their site. Having a clear watermark with your blog's name can drive more traffic and create a brand identity. Since descriptions only show up on YouTube and not other blogs where your video might be embedded, your URL can be made visible in the watermark.

Start With An Overview

Though videos are easier to watch than elaborate pieces of text, getting a user to watch an entire video is going be a challenge. How do you ensure that users are glued to your videos until the end? Simple. Just begin with an interesting overview of everything that's included in the video. This whets their appetite and keeps them hooked. This breaks the ice with your user, engages them and boosts their chances of sticking around. Get them interested and enthusiastic about what you are covering in your video. Make an interesting visual summary or map about what's coming up next. Giving them pointers about upcoming content is an excellent way to make them stay.

Create A Fantastic Call To Action

All your efforts of filming spectacular videos with the best sound and visual effects can be pointless if you do not include a compelling and impactful call to action at the end of it. Including a bright and attention-grabbing call to action ensures you don't leave your viewers high and dry after getting them interested with the video. They should know exactly what to do next if they want to know more about your products or services. Ask them to visit your website or blog or follow you on various social networks. If they sit through the entire video, they most likely are in a more positive and action oriented state of mind to follow what you tell them to do.

Optimize Your Videos

One solid tip for optimizing your YouTube videos and making them more findable is to include your main keyword in the title followed by a subtitle that lists your secondary keyword and is a rephrased version of the main title. For instance, if you have a video talking about various retirement plans, you can title as Retirement Saving Plans: 30 Brilliant Tips For Planning a Hassle-Free Retirement.

Also, ensure your video descriptions are keyword optimized, appealing, clear and descriptive. This makes it easy for search engines to place them at the top of relevant searches.

Leverage The Trailer Video Feature

If you want to convert walk-in or browse through viewers into loyal subscribers, utilize You Tube's trailer video feature optimally. The platform allows you to include a video at the top of your channel to give nonsubscribers a glimpse of your channel. This acts as a teaser to pique your audience's curiosity.

Make a compelling, sticky and appealing trailer video to bag more subscribers.

Another super layout tip is to opt for the Player view over Grid View. Unlike Grid View, Player view sets a single large video on auto-play.

Be Prolific And Upload Frequently

There are no two ways about it. If you are looking to generate passive income from your YouTube channel, you must keep adding content prolifically. The more videos you have out there and the more consistently you post these videos, the higher are your chances of creating a decent income bank. Create an editorial planner and plan to post your videos at regular intervals.

Create and upload videos that talk about different

aspects of your niche/topic/industry to build an influential channel. For example, if you run a YouTube channel related to post-pregnancy weight loss fitness regimes, try and include other related information such as healthy recipes for new mothers or post pregnancy wardrobe ideas or newborn baby care tips. Try and explore the topic from varied angles, so visitors keep coming back for more.

Chapter 4: Sell With Amazon FBA

Dropshipping is another convenient and lucrative online passive income option. A large number of virtual entrepreneurs prefer the drop shipping business model for its flexibility and simplicity. You don't need space to maintain a product inventory. Similarly, there is a minimal capital investment in setting up an e-commerce venture. While FBA (Fulfillment By Amazon) requires a flexible product investment, regular drop shipping doesn't need any upfront product investment.

The orders are fulfilled by a retail giant such as Amazon, while you get to make a tidy profit behind every sale. The best part about this business is that you can sell a huge variety of products without having to worry about maintaining a large inventory.

There's little wonder that FBA has become one of the most popular home business ventures.

FBA is a super way to leverage the power of Amazon for making profits. You do not have to deal with the sales, buyers or shipping process. Your only job is to source products and send them to Amazon for maintaining your inventory. Your products receive massive exposure in Amazon's marketplace. They store your product within their network of warehouses and deliver it to your customers. Heck, they even offer customer service. Couldn't be simpler, could it? An excellent way to rake in passive income, you say? Well yes and no. It is convenient and simple, but not a get rich overnight scheme. You need to invest considerable time and efforts in researching and identifying products that will sell like hot cakes. You will also need to find suppliers and negotiate prices with them. However, once you are all set, it can't get any more passive than this.

You literally don't have to do anything to bring in sales and deliver orders.

Upfront Costs

Unlike dropshipping, you will need a small investment to put together a product inventory for FBA and ship it to Amazon's warehouses. Other than physical product and forwarding charges, expenses you will incur include Amazon's referral fee, subscription fees (either 0.99/transaction or $39.99 monthly plan) and inventory storing fees.

The FBA calculator helps you work a selling price by considering exact fees and shipping charges. Your aim is to find unique products that people need at the right price and price them correctly to maximize your profits. The investment is completely up to the seller. You can buy products worth $10000 or $500. Start small to test your markets and scale up once you see results. Invest as much as you can afford to lose, pick your products carefully and price them judiciously.

If you are just getting your feet wet in FBA or sell more big ticket items in small quantities, you may be better off picking the $0.99/transaction subscription fee option. This plan lets you sell up to 40 products a month. However, if you reckon selling more than 40 products each month, it makes sense to sign up for the $39.99 monthly fee. This is good value for serious folks who plan to carry out hundreds of transactions each month. There are plenty of addition features, such as generating business reports in the latter.

The FBA Edge

What are the benefits of selling on FBA?

FBA items rank higher when people search for specific products. They also show up frequently on the recommended buy box option, even over items that are priced lower. Buyers are almost always likelier to opt for recommended products.

FBA products are eligible for Amazon Prime membership benefits like complimentary next day delivery, thus making Prime members much more likely to purchase these products.

You get access to a fantastic and widely used sales platform, enjoy higher search rankings, and a well-oiled, almost automated system that helps you generate huge profits consistently.

Signing Up For FBA

Start by heading to sellercentral.amazon.com. You

can either register for an FBA account with your existing credentials or create a brand new account. Pick your subscription plan depending on the number of products you expect to sell. You can either use your company's legal name or your name. Fill in your credit card number and other details. Credit card details are shared upfront so your account can be charged in the event that you run into a deficit. This can occur when you do not have any sales, yet have to bear warehouse storage and subscription fees.

Next, pick your display name. Remember, this is your brand identity. Make it unique, memorable and likable. Your audience must be able to identify and relate to it. It should be relevant to your niche if you are focusing on a specific group of products.

You will be required to confirm your identity with a phone call or text message. This completes your registration process. Fill in your bank account details so your earnings can be directly deposited into your account. The deposit method can be selected by going to the Setting tab and picking an option from the scroll down under Account Info. Verify your bank details to start receiving payments.

At this stage, you are an Amazon Seller but not yet registered for FBA. Now, visit the FBA registration page and hit on Getting Started to launch your FBA seller account.

Finding the Right Products

To begin with, you will have to be on the look-out for bargains and then measure them up against existing Amazon listings to anticipate how they will perform in comparison with competing products. How much can you sell the product for? Are the products likely to sell? Checking out existing products will answer these crucial questions. Use the Amazon Bestsellers list as a reference point to identify your star products. A product rank under rank 1000 in a relatively large category means it is faring reasonably well and can be considered for your inventory list.

Register to receive newsletter updates from reputed wholesalers or be a part of the mailing list of stores such Ikea and Walmart. They may send you special promos and offers or you can browse their website for popular or unique products. If you find a product that can be sourced really cheaply due to a limited period discount, try and order it in bulk and include it in your inventory. This way you can keep selling the product at a much higher price and rake in cool profits. Do not forget to take Amazon's fees into consideration while working out the price.

Private Label Products

Private label products are sold under your own brand name. You can source products in bulk directly from the manufacturer or wholesaler, and package the product with your label. You are therefore positioning the product as if it is being manufactured or supplied by your own firm.

Chapter 5: Create Membership Sites

Membership sites can help you rake in a good amount of passive income for a long time if you have a particular expertise that is sought after by plenty of people, especially knowledge related to the virtual world. You may be an expert in creating smartphone apps or copywriting or web designing or basically anything that people actively seek to learn. It can also be related to DIY and hobby based pursuits. How about language learning if you have mastery over a particular language or drone making if you know how to put together incredible drones?

At the onset, it is important to understand that membership sites need hard-work. You always have to keep updating, adding value, provide novel information and much more to keep your paid subscribers hooked. You must offer beyond exceptional value to retain your subscribers, which means it may not be a good option if you are just starting out in the online business world. Once you gain sufficient experience in a domain, you can consider launching your own membership site based business model. If you possess unique skills or knowledge which is in-demand, you can jump into it after doing some basic groundwork. Since information is widely available everywhere, you must have something really unique to offer your audience if you expect them to pay for it.

Adding Membership Option To Existing Blogs

If your blog is already popular among a group of readers/users who are demanding more in-depth information from you, create a membership site and give them what they are looking for. For instance, if you run a blog that gives people ideas about what topics they can blog about or blog niche ideas and your audience suggest that you also include comprehensive keywords/keyword research reports for different niches, you can charge a premium membership fee for the detailed information. If you already have a blog or website, you simply need to add a membership site plug-in to it.

Start With a Few Complimentary Slots

Start by giving out the first few slots for free to build some response and reviews for your membership based site. The most positive and active folks on your mailing list, who are always adding value in the form of suggestions or discussions, can be considered for the giveaway. You can also consider giving away the first few slots at a discounted price with a coupon mailed to your loyal subscribers.

You may have a set of people who are regularly commenting on your blog posts or social media, while also contributing meaningfully to the discussions and helping other members. Make them your evangelists. Make them feel privileged by offering them free membership, and let them spread the word about your membership site.

Focus on Creating A Loyal Community

Membership sites are as much about a supportive and loyal community feel as they are about power packed information. The information will pretty much fade away over a period of time. However, the relationship you build with your customers and the loyalty you inspire in them by adding value to their lives is what will keep them from leaving.

Membership sites are all about creating a dedicated community of users where people support each other, resolve each other's queries and offer valuable guidance. Build a passionate following on the social media, and create a learning forum where members can swap ideas and solve other's issues. Ensure that you are prompt in your response when subscribers mail you with an issue.

Always ask for feedback from active subscribers. What aspects of the topic do they want to know more about? What other tools and software they need to optimize their results? What are the most common issues they come across while doing what you teach them to? Opinion polls are a good way of identify the general sentiment related to various topics. You can build on topics that have been well-accepted and drop the ones that do not add much value.

You need to know exactly what your customers are

looking for to hand it to them on a platter. Unscreen is a handy tool for monitoring and analyzing your audience activity. It lets you know which content type is generating optimal traction so you can create more of those.

Create High-Quality build

Tutorials and guides are much sought after in today's information-packed digital world. People are looking for easier ways to perform multiple tasks. And what better to train people than to create high quality, interactive and information rich real time or pre-recorded videos. One of the biggest advantages of these videos is that they can be accessed by followers across the world according to their convenience. Ask questions, conduct polls and stimulate discussions to inspire greater user interactivity. This will keep your audience glued from start to finish.

Use high quality and evocative visuals to make the matter more interesting and digestible. Visuals can be creatively weaved into the narrative to explain tricky concepts. You need to have a rough draft of how your presentation will flow, even if you aim to keep it more spontaneous. Create a rough table of topics, which you can elaborate on during the course of the webinar. If you are catering to a more global audience, use more universally accepted words, gestures, and ideas.

Organize Your Information Efficiently

Once your site grows, you need to organize it effectively to foster better navigation and access to information for new members. Guide your members through the maze of information by putting it all together in an orderly manner. If you find that new or existing users are asking you the same questions over and over on the social media or email, you can put together a handy Q & A page for newbies.

Alternatively, have an introduction or 'begin here' page in place, where you can make new members feel less overwhelmed by all the information and guide them about navigating the available information in a step-by-step manner. Keep updating this section regularly.

Include a 'blast from the past' or 'refresher' section where you can re-post popular older blogs that members might have missed or link to those posts that are currently relevant.

Record A Friendly Welcome Video

One of the best ways to establish a warm rapport with your customers, and inspire their trust and loyalty is to record a cheery greeting video. It can be anything from a demonstration of how the site works or a story or a gentle reminder of the do's and don'ts. You can tell them how they can make optimal utilization of your services or how they can contact you should they stumble upon some issues or inspiring experiences of existing members.

Bring In The Influencers

You can offer free subscriptions to authoritative figures in your industry and ask them to leave behind genuine reviews about the site. People are likelier to take their unbiased report seriously, and give your site a look through. Since influencers have a relatively large follower base, your site will enjoy a wide reach among potential subscribers.

Create Group Events

Group events and challenges are a great way to engage existing members and keep them hooked. Motivate them and help them stay on track. It can be anything small like a challenge that helps subscribers attain a specific goal. For instance, if you run a membership site for writers who aspire to fulfill their writing goals, create a challenge video that encourages subscribers to complete a goal for the week. The buzz of working as a group/community can be wonderfully motivating and creates a strong, positive vibe. You can also have other events, team challenges (where members compete with each other), courses and similar activities frequently to keep your subscribers on their toes.

CONCLUSION

Thanks for making it through to the end of this book, let's hope it was informative and able to provide you with all of the tools you need to achieve your goals whatever they may be.

The next step is to apply everything that you have

learned about options trading. So, open an account today and rake in serious profits.

About The Author

Hi there it's Jonathan Walker here, I want to share a little bit about myself so that we can get to know each other on a deeper level. I grew up in California, USA, and have lived there for the better part of my life. Being exposed to many different people and opportunities when I was young, it made me want to strive to become an entrepreneur to escape the rat race path that most of my peers had taken. I knew I wanted to be able to travel and experience the world the way it was meant to be seen and I've done just that. I've travelled to most places around the world and I'm enjoying every minute of it for sure. In my free time I love to play tennis and believe it or not, compose songs. I wish you all the best again in your endeavours, and may your dreams, whatever they may be, come true abundantly in the near future.

www.ingramcontent.com/pod-product-compliance
Lightning Source LLC
LaVergne TN
LVHW010326070526
838199LV00065B/5672